Anne Frank

Sandra Woodcock

Published in association with The Basic Skills Agency

Hodder & Stoughton

A MEMBER OF THE HODDER HEADLINE GROUP

Acknowledgements

Photos: pp. 3, 11, 15, 20, 23 and 25 © AKG photo,
        pp. 9 and 28 © Corbis-Bettmann.
Cover photo: © AKG photo.

Orders: please contact Bookpoint Ltd, 39 Milton Park, Abingdon, Oxon OX14 4TD. Telephone: (44) 01235 400414, Fax: (44) 01235 400454. Lines are open from 9.00–6.00, Monday to Saturday, with a 24 hour message answering service. You can also order through our website www.hodderheadline.co.uk

British Library Cataloguing in Publication Data
A catalogue record for this title is available from The British Library

ISBN 0 340 71160 4

First published 1998
Impression number 10 9 8 7 6 5 4
Year 2003

Typeset by Fakenham Photosetting Ltd, Fakenham, Norfolk.
Printed in Great Britain for Hodder & Stoughton Educational, a division of Hodder Headline 338 Euston Road, London NW1 3BH by Bath Press, Bath

Contents

What is it like to live in fear?
What is it like to have to hide away
to save your life?
What is it like to stay indoors
for two long years?
What is it like to see hell on earth?

Most of us will never know.
But Anne Frank knew all of this.
She was just a teenager.
She dreamed of being famous.
She put pictures of film stars on her wall.
She fell out with her mother
and she wrote all this in her diary.

But Anne Frank was not an ordinary teenager.
She was a Jew
and her life was always in danger.

1 Germany

Anne Frank was born in June 1929.
She had one older sister called Margot.
Her family lived in Frankfurt in Germany.
They were German Jews.

Anne's father, Otto, had been an officer
in the Germany army in World War 1.
The family were well off
and their life in Germany was happy.
But that would not last long.

Soon after Anne was born,
hard times came to Germany.
The German people turned to the Nazi party.
The Nazi party grew stronger day by day.

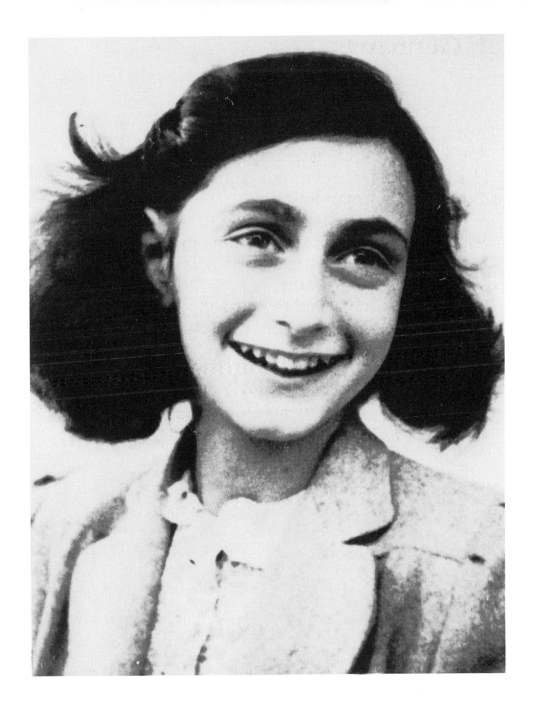

In 1933 Adolf Hitler
became leader of Germany.
Germany was now a dangerous place for Jews.
Hitler and the Nazis hated the Jews.
They began to bully the Jews.
They made Jews give up their jobs.

A lot of Jews said things would get worse.
It was better to leave Germany.
Otto Frank made up his mind to go.
He took his family to Holland
to start a new life.

2 A New Life

Otto Frank started a new business
in Amsterdam.
It was a small family business.
The people who worked for him
said he was a good man.
They liked working for him.
They felt as if they were
part of his family.

The Frank family
got on well with their neighbours.
Some were German refugees like them.
Others were Dutch.

The children settled down to their new life.
Margot was hard working and quiet.
Anne was only four
when they came to Holland.
She was very lively and full of fun.

She went to school
and in the next few years
she made many friends.
She liked to be at the centre of things.
She liked attention.

She was a child who liked
to say what she was thinking.
Some adults said she was too bold.
One mother said:
'God knows everything,
but Anne knows everything better.'

The Frank family were doing well.
But in Germany,
Hitler had made plans for war.
In 1939 he went to war, and by 1940
the Germans had taken over most of Europe.
Otto Frank said the Germans
would not invade Holland.
But he was wrong.

In May 1940 Holland was taken over.
Now the Jews in Holland
had to obey Nazi laws.
Jews were not allowed in swimming pools.
Jews were not allowed to go to the cinema.
Jews had to shop at certain times.
At 8pm all Jews had to be in their homes.
Every Jew had to wear a badge.
It was a yellow star.

The Jews put up with all of this.
But Otto was worried that
things might get worse.
In secret, he began to make a hiding place
for his family.

Otto's business was in a big house
by a canal.
He made the secret hiding place
in some of the rooms
at the top of the house.
He began to collect furniture
and cooking things.

Anne's 13th birthday was on 12 June 1942.
She had some friends for a party at home.
Her father rented a film for them to see.

One of Anne's presents was a diary.
She loved the idea of keeping a diary.
When she wrote in it,
she pretended she was writing to a friend.
She called the friend Kitty.
So she always began 'Dear Kitty . . .'

In her diary, she wrote
like any other 13 year old.
She wrote gossip about her friends
and what was going on at school.
She wrote down her feelings
about growing up and the way her body
was changing.

All Jews in Amsterdam knew
that the Nazis were taking Jews to Germany
to work in labour camps.
They all lived in fear.
One Sunday, on 5 July 1942,
a letter came for Anne's sister.
Margot Frank had to go to Germany.
Otto knew that it was time
to go to the secret hiding place.

The family left their home in a hurry.
They made up a story
that they were going to Switzerland.

Some pages from Anne Frank's diary.

3 In Hiding

When the Frank family came to the office,
they went upstairs.
In one small room there was a bookcase.
The bookcase hid a secret door.
Behind the door there were some stairs.
The stairs led to the secret rooms.

There were five secret rooms.
At first there were
seven people living there:
the Frank family and three friends,
Mr and Mrs Van Daan and their son Peter.
Later another Jew came to hide there.
So there were eight of them.

That first day,
Anne's mother and her sister sat on the bed.
They looked sad and tired.
But Anne and her father were busy,
setting things up and sorting out the rooms.

Anne shared a room with her sister.
She put up all her pictures of film stars
on the bare walls.

But Anne was cheerful as well,
and tried to make the best of it.
She read a lot and talked to Peter Van Daan.
He said that she cheered him up.
They became very fond of each other.
For a time she was in love with him:

'I have the feeling now
that Peter and I share a secret.
If he looks at me with those eyes
that laugh and wink,
then it's just as if a little light
goes on inside me.'

The news from outside was often bad.
More Jews were taken away.
They knew that many of them would die.
They knew about concentration camps.
Anne wrote in her diary about a nightmare.
In her dream she saw an old school friend
in a concentration camp.

The bookcase and secret door.

Otto told only the four people
who worked for him.
No-one else was told where they had gone.
The people who worked for Otto brought food,
books and other things every day.
One of the women was called Miep.
Anne wrote about her in her diary.
She came to see them every day
and told them what was happening outside.

They all lived in hiding for two years.
In her diary Anne wrote about her life.
At times it was very hard.
They had to keep the blinds closed
at all times.
They could only flush the toilet
when the office workers had gone home,
in case anyone heard them.
They had to walk about very quietly.

At first they were glad to be safe.
But as time went on,
they all felt the strain of never going out.
Anne's diary tells how
she fell out with the others.
There were rows about food and money.
Anne wrote down her angry feelings
about most of the people she lived with.

She would row with her mother:

'I'm boiling with rage,
and yet I mustn't show it.
I'd like to stamp my feet, scream,
give Mummy a good shaking ...'

Anne and her mother did not get on well.
Anne said in her diary
that Margot was too soft,
and always let people talk her round.
Anne wanted to be stronger.
She spoke her mind and did not give in.
But she felt as if
people were always finding fault with her.

Sometimes she felt very low:

'My nerves often get the better of me ...
you don't hear a bird singing outside
and a deadly close silence hangs everywhere,
catching hold of me
as if it will drag me down
deep into an underworld.'

4 Hope

They all tried to keep up with the war news.
They listened to radio news from England.
At last, in June 1944,
they heard some good news.
British and American soldiers
had landed in France.
They were going to drive the Germans out.

This was a time of great hope.
The British and American armies
would free all of Europe from the Nazis.
Otto Frank had a map.
He marked on it the movements of the armies,
as they won ground from the Germans.

On 21 July 1944, Anne wrote in her diary:

'Now I am getting really hopeful,
now things are going really well at last.'

But the Jews in hiding
were not as safe as they thought.
The Nazis needed more and more Jews
to work for Germany.
In Holland there were rewards for people
who helped to find Jews in hiding.

5 Betrayed

Someone told the police in Amsterdam
that there were Jews hiding
in Otto Frank's office building.

On 4 August 1944,
four policemen turned up at the building.
They knew where to look.
They went straight to the bookcase.
They arrested all eight people
and took them to the Gestapo prison.

They also took all the things
they could carry from the hiding place.
They did not take Anne's diary.

After they had gone,
Miep who had helped the family,
found the diary on the floor.
She took it away and kept it safe.

Miep went to the Gestapo prison,
to beg for them to be set free.
But there was no chance.
After a few days
they were all moved on to a work camp.

Now the Nazis were taking Jews to Poland
to camps where they would work or die.
One of the biggest camps was Auschwitz.
Many trains left for Auschwitz,
loaded with Jews.
On 3 September 1944, the last train left.
The Frank family and their friends were on it.

6 Hell on Earth

The journey to Auschwitz took three days.
The train was packed full
of men, women and children.
There was no room to lie down.
People had to sleep standing up,
or on their knees.
There were no toilets.
It was hard to breathe.

The train arrived at Auschwitz
on 6 September 1944.
The men and women were separated.
Then the old and the weak,
the sick and young children
were sent to the gas chambers
and they were killed.

The Nazis were only interested
in Jews who could work.
Those who could work
were sent to the barracks.

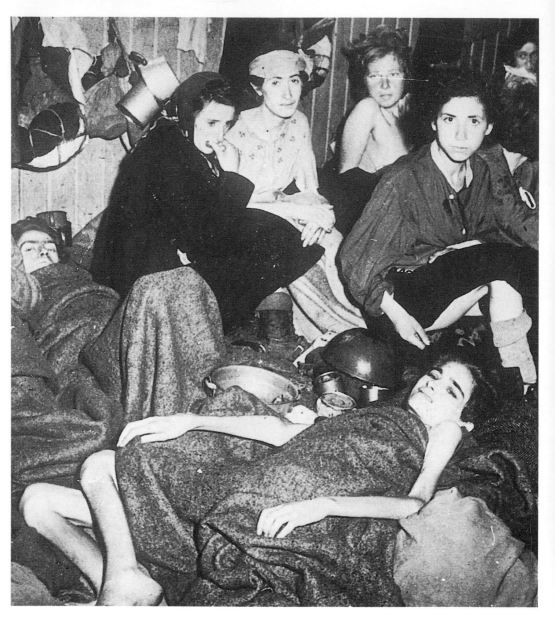

Hell on earth.

Anne, her mother and her sister
were alive and still together.
But they had come to a place
that was hell on earth.

All over the camp was the smell
of burning flesh, smoke and disinfectant.
Those who were kept alive to work
were weak and cold and had little food.
They were only just alive.
The Nazis treated them very badly.

In October, Anne and her sister
were moved again.
This time they were sent to Bergen-Belsen,
another concentration camp.
Their mother was left behind in Auschwitz.
She died there two months later
from starvation.

When Anne and Margot came to Bergen-Belsen,
there were not enough barracks
for all the new Jews to stay in.
Many of them were given tents to sleep in.
But there were strong winds and cold rain.
The tents were blown away
and these Jews were left with only blankets
in a very bad storm.

Anne and Margot met some friends
from Amsterdam, other Jews who
had been found by the Nazis.
Anne and Margot
did get into the barracks at last.
But they had the bottom bunk,
right next to the door.
The freezing winds
blew right on to them all winter.

Helping the survivors of Bergen-Belsen.

They were weak and always hungry.
They were covered in lice.
There was a disease called typhus
in the camp.
All around them women were sick and dying.
They believed both their parents were dead.
They began to give up hope.

Margot was very ill.
She became weaker and weaker,
and at last she died.
Now Anne was all alone.
The war was nearly over.
The Germans were losing.
Soon the camps would be found
and the Jews who survived would be free.

But it was not soon enough for Anne.
She died in 1945,
one month before British soldiers
got to Bergen-Belsen.
Her thin body was probably thrown on a pile
of other bodies in the mass graves there.

A mass grave at Bergen-Belsen.

7 The Diary

Of the eight people
who had been in hiding together,
only one lived to see the end of the war.
Otto Frank was set free from Auschwitz
in January 1945.
He was very ill, but he was alive.

He went back to Holland
and tried to find news of his family.
He found out that his wife had died
but he hoped the girls were still alive.
But at last he had news
that they were both dead.

Now Miep came to him with Anne's diary.
She had not read it,
and she did not give it to Otto
until she knew Anne was dead.
Otto did not know what to do with it.
Friends told him he must publish the diary,
so that the world would know Anne's story.

Anne had talked about publishing her diary
after the war.
She had always said she wanted to be famous.
So Otto did publish her diary,
and Anne had her wish.

The diary has sold over 25 million copies.
It has been translated
into more than 50 languages.

A play was made about Anne's life.
There have been films too.
Her father said
that he only really knew Anne
after he had read her diary.

Millions of other people
have got to know Anne Frank in the same way.
The house in Amsterdam
with its secret hiding place
can still be seen today.
People from all over the world go to see it.

They think of Anne Frank.

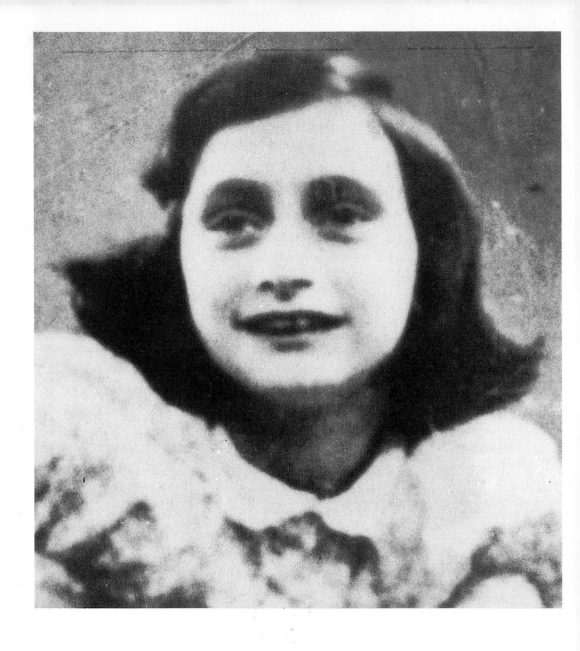